PRAISE FOR *WINTER PHOENIX*

What language can we use to describe atrocities mounting on top of atrocities? How do we organize the telling? What happens after? In Sophia Terazawa's stunning and necessary debut collection of poetry, we begin with the letter A, we begin in Vietnam. We climb a hill. On our journey we encounter different systems and schema for representing "the moment of slaughter" (the affidavit, the cross-examination, the grease work and its diagrams, the Pleiades, the Q and A). But we do not progress as much as watch events disperse like light through a prism. "Therefore, we direct that length of earth through weed then bone, using this meter of our killers . . ." writes Terazawa. "Yes, we thus decompose to open gaps for breath . . ." Terazawa splinters, she reconstitutes, we witness the burn, the rise. There's a limit to what can happen in a colonial language. In *Winter Phoenix*, Terazawa takes us beyond it.

—Susan Briante, author of *Defacing the Monument*

I envy you, who are about to experience Sophia Terazawa's *Winter Phoenix*, for the jagged, life-harrowing testimony / the searing counterautopsy performed on the overspreading shadows of human extremity / and the enforced contortions and yet finally free revelations of language / that are about to incite and irrevocably transform your mind and especially your heart. Terazawa's poetry—trial, exhibition, demonstration, transfiguration, ballad of descendant unquiet—is the hardest won form of love. It is poetry as refoliation.

—Brandon Shimoda, author of *The Grave on the Wall*

Violence looks back, tries to find quiet in its wake, but quiet chooses instead to slip away to a place Elias Khoury called Little Mountain. Toni Morrison took us to the clearing. Paul Celan followed ashes into the sky. Like them, Sophia Terazawa leans closer to the page, to its ink, deeper into the chest and throat, closer to the edges of her fingertips, so she can lift quiet into the imagination and thereby inaugurate a courtroom for reckoning, a chamber for transformation, a hill for a tattered flag, and a hill again, to run down, arms open, holding out an amulet of love.

—Farid Matuk, author of *The Real Horse*

Sophia Terazawa's profound debut collection, *Winter Phoenix*, invites us to seek out radical healing rituals as a means to persevere amidst the horrors of empire during the Vietnam War. Beneath its testimonies, exhibits, cross-examinations, and diagrams of war crime tribunals is the incantation of voices that can no longer remain unheard. The poet honors these voices that span "between documents and justice," along with the ancestral and astral, toward greater possibilities of repair. By conjuring an inquiry of these crimes, by subverting language of the empire, and by seeking new accountability, the reader is compelled to not look away but then to ask: where does complicity end and healing begin? This collection guides us to listen deeper and encourages us to consider who speaks and is allowed to speak, who jurors the justice and receives the justice, who can and cannot answer the questions to make us whole. In its refusal to "Learn to / spēk / just how this / ˈkəntrē / speaks," we are pushed further so that within these pages transformation becomes all the more possible.

—Anthony Cody, author of *Borderland Apocrypha*

With *Winter Phoenix*, Sophia Terazawa conducts a symphony of voices, documents, and archives in the form of lyric testimonies which bring to mind precedent texts such as Charles Reznikoff's *Testimony*, Layli Long Soldier's *Whereas*, and M. NourbeSe Philip's *Zong!* Incisive and microscopic, Terazawa examines the intimacies of the unnamed speaker's matrilineal line while cross-examining those who were complicit in war crimes during the Resistance War Against America, or American War, or the "Vietnam War" (as it is referred to outside of Vietnam). Lush ecological textures and "[h]ills of lemongrass and eucalyptus" juxtapose against lyric redactions and source materials: "Well, I've shot deer and I've gutted deer. It was just like when you stick a deer with a knife—sort of a thud—or something like this, sir," culminating in searing treatise against and indictment of war. Terazawa is exacting in her visions of the personal and transnational past. "These facts are very simple," she writes, and she's absolutely right—but the aftermath, the legacy—is far from it.

—Diana Khoi Nguyen, author of *Ghost of*

WINTER

TESTIMONIES IN VERSE

PHOENIX

WINTER

PHOENIX

TESTIMONIES IN VERSE

SOPHIA TERAZAWA

DEEP VELLUM

DALLAS, TX

Deep Vellum Publishing
3000 Commerce St., Dallas, Texas 75226
deepvellum.org · @deepvellum

Deep Vellum is a 501c3 nonprofit literary arts organization founded in 2013 with the mission to bring the world into conversation through literature.

Support for this publication has been provided in part by grants from the Moody Fund for the Arts and the Amazon Literary Partnership:

ISBNs: 978-1-64605-142-7 (paperback) | 978-1-64605-143-4 (ebook)

LIBRARY OF CONGRESS CATALOGING-IN-PUBLICATION DATA

Names: Terazawa, Sophia, author.
Title: *Winter phoenix : testimonies in verse* / Sophia Terazawa.
Description: Dallas : Deep Vellum, 2021.
Identifiers: LCCN 2021025789 | ISBN 9781646051427 (trade paperback) | ISBN
    9781646051434 (ebook)
Subjects: LCSH: Vietnam War, 1961-1975--Poetry. | War crimes--Poetry. |
    LCGFT: Poetry.
Classification: LCC PS3620.E736 W56 2021 | DDC 811/.6--dc23
LC record available at https://lccn.loc.gov/2021025789

Cover Design and Interior Layout by David Wojciechowski · www.davidwojo.com

PRINTED IN THE UNITED STATES OF AMERICA

CONTENTS

ALLEGATIONS

BYLAWS

MORNING CEREMONY

CLOSING STATEMENT   133

PREFACE

This volume, one of many, is intended for the present moment, more specifically, the American English language used to justify its country's crimes against humanity.

While the source material originates from soldiers' testimonies given during three internationally publicized events, in this order—*The Incident on Hill 192* (1966, Phù Mỹ District, Vietnam), *The Winter Soldier Investigation* (1971, Detroit, USA), and *The Russell Tribunal* (1966, Stockholm, Sweden; 1967, Roskilde, Denmark)—*Winter Phoenix* is, in actuality, about the ongoing survival as the daughter of my mother.

KEY TERMS, INDIRECT TRANSLATIONS

●—	*"A"*
Alcyone	*Goddess; Star System*
/ Bäm /	*"Bomb"*
Diacritics	*Tonal Markers (i.e., nhà; nhá)*
Làm Sao	*Why; How*
Miscanthus	*Elephant Grass*
Nước	*Country; Water*
果	*Fruit*
Quan Âm	*O, Lady of Sweet Mercy*
Bertrand Russell	*Western Philosopher*
Sa Huỳnh	*Iron Age*
/ ˈWiTHər /	*"Whither"*

*I WROTE THIS BOOK OF JUSTICE
THEN OUR AMULET OF LOVE.*

OPERATION PHOENIX

If we start a burial, the ceremony larger than its copper
parts combined—this other side, some bovine horn of us—
what punctuating earth might rectify an addressee or incidental
crime, I'd prophesize a little, that which spoke unknowingly.

The throat might signal *throat* or *ram* against his set of fork-
split eyes. To turn this name of both our wars becoming *egg*
of blood rite after blood, beloved, would you rise up from this
country of our killers? No, our ram and bovine horn in sacrifice

inverting one more testimony, comrade, spells no jurisdiction
in this ritual of justice without justice; what may lend our body
as its torch, the possibility of saying, *No*, in four or five separate
languages, our amulet of copper and my double-headed stone.

OPENING STATEMENT

17 NOVEMBER 1966

Morning. Uphill 192, the chicken bone as jute made durative and marked
attached to nail reduced to bones in place of grass, that month turned into spoons,
a bar of soap, exhibits *A* through—evidently bent around her body—marks
of which we couldn't speak by. Then we felt for loops. A loop fell down
leaving its print. To kneel around or name her body—*here* and *there*; to testify
which lung inverted, *here* or *there*, deducing what was brown would happen
on that hill. *I was alone, mama.* Why did you stand there and say nothing?

WITNESS OATH (1)

That place, then our syllable for skin, became one room, two intersecting walls; sliding across, two mirrors tall as men who entered, and they watched. I would awake. I was awakened, after that, was bruised then filmed or made to bark like dog(s). I don't remember much. It happened, yes. Their women watched. They also laughed. I was therefore their dog(s). Yes, solemnly I swear, what happened on that hill would happen in this room four decades later. Why did you just stand there and say nothing?

18 NOVEMBER 1966

Yes, we swore to tell that truth—retribution, not a subject
                              likening to waves of bullets

running through my arms. You wrecked into it, falling,
                              altered light, at best.

Pacing in circles, near us, there, we found a stag. That stag was tall
                              and wounded, bleeding downhill.

Edges raveled to our dips of earth made, once again, too red.
                              That hill had bloomed.

At this, we wanted then, to end. Yesterday, horns were upside down,
                              and ramming, bleated days.

We made a month to swear by—
                              Yes, we ran. I ran. That woman ran.

These women died. I did not die. The only difference, here, is—somewhere,
                              in our country—one might call this

patience. Yes, we testified.
                              Justice carving figs into a date—

the only difference, here, is—somehow, I survived.

EXPATRIATED FUGUE

You shouldn't have to / ˈwiTHər / when you come here / sed / the papers at arrival. Take / igˈzampəl / from persimmons hanging in an / ˈôrCHərd / ˈhevē / with late autumn. Herein lies a / ˈsiNGgəl / motion: fell them near their trunks using whatever / nīf / you came with, toss it / (h)wen / you're / dən / and / ˈmōSH(ə)n / once again to / ˈdemənˌstrāt / how you arrived / ˌənˈärmd / because the papers / sed / you should, expatriate: a pairing of / too͞ / syllables in motion. Learn to / spēk / just how this / ˈkəntrē / speaks. You shouldn't have to / kəm / up with your words, an orchard or its noun flickering / (h)wen / you strike the fruit or take example. Hanging / bī / ə / stem for all your countrymen to / sē / you wither down / ə / ˈCHes(t)ˌnət / red to brown / ə / nīf / which I will / ˈberē / when you work into me, too.

WITNESS OATH (2)

Then a stag circled my body. When I woke, I had no shoes.

      Facing the stag, I brayed.

Men would come
      to pick me up

Then take us other places.

      Placed inside a room, I fell, was made to fall.

      I'm sorry that this happened.

      Why did you just stand there and say nothing?

      If we wanted then to find—

      Our door would open. Men would enter.

      Who confessed to no one? No one was my hero.

after Phan Thi Mao

19 NOVEMBER 1966

Yes, confessing we were brown and young, belonging to that epilogue of rote-
required memory, I was that young. Suspended, hitting gavels with our tongue.

Or ordering of roses, buttoned to a chest, what made to soften, yes, they took us
out. Battalions had left. We couldn't leave. They'd let us go. I ran into the bush.

Ahead of us, your name was also mine because of this. I was too young,
corralling hands in counting ways to take us back, before that war—

that statement on our hill, dislodged beside her name—that woman, running
out then in, withholding arms, for she was shot before they called her young.

Our trials happened but we never happened. Yes, speaking in languages
through us, mama, I was that young without her name, decaying on her hill.

That start of us, a song—"Chúng tôi lớn lên mỗi người mỗi ngả!"
—burned up a flag of red, we placed inside our hands, standing for love.

after Tế Hanh

WITNESS OATH (3)

Stars inside my mouth, I placed a star

      Then made of clay, was therefore red.

      Men stood in place, then changing

      Places, left our room.

      Staggering
I recall his palm against the next, each man

      Slapping high-fives therefore passing through

      Men changing place.

         I knelt again

Then stood.

We knelt again, that star turning to gold.

after you, mama

HILL 192

Well, I've shot deer and I've gutted deer. It was just like when you stick a deer with a knife—sort of a thud—or something like this, sir.

"Sven Eriksson"
Honorably Discharged (1968)

"WE ARE READY TO LET THE TESTIMONY SAY IT ALL."

Lt. William Crandell, "Opening Statement"
Winter Soldier Investigation (1971)

I.

Morale:

The peach light at a bend—

1700, awoken to the baboons hooting
        cruel as thrush, jungle, frond.

Search:

Non- (search, noun)

Search (plume)—shoot anything that moves.

Meaning, a girl was taken from her hamlet
        then into our jungle where (thrush)

my mother followed.

II.

Dormant fauna
   we had crossed
blue rusting up

     its algae, ochre
marrow
     bloomed. I pushed us
   through.

Morale:

   That purpose of *bloom-bloom*—

   Meaning, affront or frond
that squad of mud
       I was therefore your sister.

III.

Roaring grass

Vermillion was there-

Fore wood or thorn that

Vine grazing our feet,

We chose to walk uphill.

IV.

I closed myself, wherefore that

Body should be felt inside another

Something close to human, red-

Divine and glowing cyclothymic

Wings of dark eyes moth, that

Whistle calling forth its dead—

Peeling from lips, a spotted fawn
    thus roaring.

V.

Capgras:

Wherefore doubled over—

I had begged
　　　　such daughter's affidavit.

Capgras:

Wherefore mouth was stuffed into—

That drowning affidavit
　　　　took this cloth and stuffed in two—

War Logic:

Wherefore incidents were lauded
manning,
　　　　who stepped forward,
　　we absolved.

VI.

Beyond that scope of human law,
how lively we became.

     To summon strength, confession,
    or some names, how gentle were you

searching for that name to lap
    inside of me.

    I marched in two
    circling
bà ngoại looking down.

I wanted you to see her, too.

VII.

You touching, no, that blushing tropic rose

Đà Lạt of rose, that blushing noun

Participating in its graze—

Carefully what would run

That M-16 as caption, crushed this end to us.

I wonder what you know. I wondered

What you knew. Why did you stand there

And say nothing?

VIII.

That jam, jutted, and fend-for

Crawled our bacchanal of soil

Slain in front of you that highland

Ever-changing lime, chartreuse

Of fern running-ravine, where after

All you should have known we

Did not sound like that. Why did

You stand there and say nothing?

IX.

Mountain or
of opaline horizon
           bayoneted. They were gentle.

At first we were gentle.

Through one thigh, that shoulder
                had no use,
                          our ream of stars.

What loving crucifixion we attempted.

Anyway, that basilisk
circled her carcass.

X.

Back to fawn—
    what we may never know,

that reverb
    meeting spirit,

golden alabaster trauma
    broken into pale

soft-spoken rivers—
    how we whet and also

how we whet
    meeting our spirit

swallowed through
    its basilisk, its fawn

therefore an egg
    we spotted at a striding

line—that seam of which
    made taut, yes,

back to fawn, we stood there
    but said nothing.

XI.

Lest I flood, and lest that sound roar out of me
    becoming animal, that animal of tongue.

Lest haunted by its ruin, what could break
    though light then canopy of frond, I'd live beyond

you, sister. What may therefore carry we then
    curl like a trial; though that trial, make its tongue.

I live beyond you, sister. Let me try.

TESTIMONY A ["ABSOLUTELY VIRTUOUS"]

MODERATOR: Can you tell us—

Yes. That absolution of a virtue must begin with concrete, oak, and textured pronouns—*we, beginning* as a layout, mounds of dirt first climbing, up then out, through military terms—we measure that which comes too close to us—that *Hill One-Ninety-Two*—in other words, what multiplies our voice beneath its meter, voices running downhill? How do trials make another body absent? Therefore, we direct that length of earth through weed then bone, using this meter of our killers—*a, b, c*—you understand this, sir. Yes, we thus decompose to open gaps for breath, to readjust our weight, to make too monumental—*crime, becoming*, finally, itself because we said it so—*women, hunted*, were first shot then stabbed—each comma, here, most crucial to our story, hence, delineating men from action during war—a woman, hunted, was then killed upon another hill. These facts are very simple.

CROSS-EXAMINATION (A.1)

Absolutely, we were frightened by that absence

when / əˈnəTHər / told / ə / story of our mouths

refracting one more / bäm / to harvest pain

upon virtue, alone,
this adjective—and in
some cases, adverb—

what was lost in / ˈsimpəl / terms.

We left without
speaking a word
most commonly
archaic—*noun*,
that core of

which dropped barrels stuffed with herbicidal rage.

/ Pərˈ(h)aps / preceding us, one ballad to each tongue,

oh, / ˈabsəˌl(y)o͞otlē /, we refrained from singing.

EXHIBIT (A.1)

What rooted us a ruby
hardened sphere in fact

before or after

pausing leaving tint
granular dark

around our scar

the woman lifting
up her skirt or saying

it looks bad a little

bad and there's a
doctor somewhere

who could

look at this
she means if only

guava seed

our older species
turning into grain.

CROSS-EXAMINATION (A.2)

Grief for textual / igˈzampəl /

we wept / ˈōpənlē / as for another

fifty years would need us calm

and / ärmd / with readiness.

A hundred kilograms of wings had grown anew.
A feather wedged into another broken vertebra.

We sang regarding what pronounced itself / ə / body.

Help us understand the nature of this crime.
We did not need your help—

oh, / ˈānjəl / of sweet mercy.

EXHIBIT (A.2)

First, the woman squatted, gnawing
at a piece of skin stuck to her golden
tooth, dislodged, then clothed,
a tunic for her molar, silk-white
pair of trousers for its miniature thighs.

Secondly, she started eating and then
whimpering a mirror into pieces. Then
we sank it all, what turned into this wheel
what fell down spineless to the ground
next to another wheel. A crocus bloomed.

We plucked that tooth which billowed
out her circle, testifying what would
happen next: a burning on its wire
or the map of it, our circular red
mirror knocked down by the crocus.

CROSS-EXAMINATION (A.3)

/ (H)wət / else could we call our missing court of law or scale of justice

scabbing at / ə / valley filled with crocuses / ə / ˈkwīət / saffron moving

crimson tenfold over rank and power scrub of meadows devastating?

Who was drawn already through the wound and through each moving hour?
Who was devastated not through touch but wanting desperately for that moment—

/ˈaftər / which she made herself / ə / glass of boiling extract

which we pinched between / ə / set of plateaus luminously lyric.

What was conjured? Rouge attesting to our future weaponry of beauty.

/ (H)wət / else could we find there—red-boned like some lesser god?

EXHIBIT (A.3)

Une pomme một quả
roots in Sino-Vietnamese

apiece the black car ruin.
果 in Hà Nội (kwa) or (wa)

of Sài Gòn's *angel*. Quan
Âm help us *merci trop*.

That catalog of sound
between us blew an apple

grove apart our diplomatic
man inside his diplomatic

vehicle. We stood there
and inside of that another.

TESTIMONY B ["TENDING TO HER BUFFALO"]

MODERATOR: Can you tell us—

Yes. Her only crime was that she led her buffalo across his field, your firing of questions: *What would happen next?*—you'd never understand it, sir, or understand our language, or in whispering, the farmer named her *Bò*; that *B* standing for *Beg* using a *Bayonet*—or atrophy by bayonet—an ongoing of nouns, for instance, blue marble would jut into the mountains: Bovine, Bending, Backward. Hooves pressed into earth, and horns became our rivulet of sound. What happened next? She said, *I'm tending to my Bò.* So why did you just stand there and say nothing?

EXHIBIT (B.1)

After green the color stained
a tangling of tussock grass.

Before that aster-brown
concealed us, in frame, astro-

nomic citizens of knowing.
After this a banyan blurred

and after that a tenderizing
speech subtitled, out of focus

talismanic bullhorns filled in
after you, blue clay and banyan

limbs rotating with their breeze.
I filmed that, too. Beloved,

where you stood by uttering
an *O*—, mid-archive like a photo-

graphic gurgle. That was easy
but the globular colliding into

two disjointed parts. I was
then the girl, and then I was

that braying buffalo alone
inside his field over the body

of my wife. Why did you just
stand there and say nothing?

CROSS-EXAMINATION (B.1)

Con Trâu: bulls belonging to erasure
we pronounced them, *semi-automatic*. You were missing, my beloved.

In the center of our conflict, Con Trâu
lobbed his chubby body past each armament of power.

Or that river delta stripped its ivory-white crocus, I then needed to protect my Bò
and not the other way around.

Forgive me, Bò.

: northern glottal stop.
: a terminal conjunction damming up this highland.
: what would run but could not run.
: across her field, the farmer's only crime.

I stood there but said nothing.

And the dream:
Con Trâu:

Using his body as a shield:

CROSS-EXAMINATION (B.2)

Chân Này, but belonging to one Riverine:

That / bī / and / bī / beneath his whirring gray ma-
chine
/ bloō / zoned our braying Chân Này under fire.

Operative's Ad Nauseum, Mobile Afloat:

That force of which figured his delta / bī / butane-
black
liquid dust, beloved, you were spoken for.

EXHIBIT (B.2)

Barreling down
operative quadrants
what blew off

then vomited
to sing out, "Sừng
của một con vật!"

to bind our river
buffalo somewhere
inside this marsh,

to stumble out
regardless, bolting
on a set of fractured

knees, the buffalo
had screamed
then flung himself

between the girl
and soldier like
his bones could hold

no water. You were
there, ma, streaked
with mud and gold.

TESTIMONY C ["OPEN CAVITY"]

MODERATOR: Can you tell us—

Colon. Over there, a woven basket lined with glass commenced; whoever did this did not think; that is a generous assumption rising up its cranial contusion. Pulled out of its trial, for example, colloid fraying into bits, this *open cavity*, stopping at the sternum and your Budweiser nearby. Who ordered this? Who ordered this to happen?

EXHIBIT C

How strips of cloth ripped out of mud spoke through us,
sheltering its carnage; how a coda carefully inflamed

carved through us like fermata; what would come for
torso, larynx, femur? Anyway, discretely, mental nouns

skinned every clarity of speech. Attraction cast us end-
lessly unwashed and scrubbed, corroded of our spikes.

Removing carefully, the cavalry of copper—*Over there*,
we screamed, *don't touch her!*—instantly we peeled,

commenced red conical adaption, cavities like commas
culled mnemonically, forced into containment, carried

by its stomach, sacs of corn—the apparatus—daily
amniotic, for withal, remaining of a body, we could

run on endlessly, the words for this. There is no other
word for this—what has been done to her—the woman

running up a hill then falling through its overgrowth
—her hair, that fan staining a wind too black against

our face, the pouring out of language—*No, comrade*,
we left a crocus. What could ever prove that slaughter

misplaced stones with justice? No, we took this nail.
And then we took the glass to make anew her home.

TESTIMONY D ["F-4 PHANTOM"]

MODERATOR: Can you tell us—

In this way, I dared it to happen: a document darting between you and a premise for postcombat interview, in other words, divorce—*stock footage: cumulus*—what eddied along the delta, an incident or nineteen-ton machine making its diagram of clouds, bridge by smoldering bridge, and of our phantom, you said, exchanging this dawn for something else—*stock footage: illegible*—we looked like history, but leaving the desert, you wouldn't say goodbye.

EXHIBIT D

Which desiccation dared
another phantom to announce
reflective years which
flattened down an open mouth
which darted up then scathed
our air made seamlessly
too beige which flew down
tendered by this cadence
of some war we never wanted.

Which we sent back
joining diacritic marks
in dialogue of old colonial
respectabilities which deigned
our genocide which dared
to speak of dignity then
freedom that which
slaughtered in one breath
our people then our land.

The facts of this were simple.
Once we spoke for independence
bodies were then marked
then punctuated by an order
that which drowned out
that which coding fields
made livestock out of us and
that which would defoliate
another nation turning fists
which rose up like a bird.

CROSS-EXAMINATION D

Khi Nào: Centuries would pass without our knowing.

> Crying out, these hundred
> faces left behind.

Làm Sao: Pistons curling in dark and metal chambers.

> There, what dreadfully reframed
> an interface of documents.

One held a photograph of smoke.
Another colored sheaves.

> Our eyes in black, for we were there
> two hundredfold.

One could not grieve.
One held to questions or response, though never both.

> You understand that, sir.

TESTIMONY E ["E-TOOL"]

MODERATOR: Can you tell us—

Yes. We wondered how the portable entrenching tool, responsible for balancing a rock with grounds for termination, simply stood there like a man propped up against his work. The work: a juniper.

The disassembling of root from bone: what task force called this, *rounding up* instead of *making for*—its massacre, an ornamental sound? The tree falls in a forest, and nobody makes her sound.

CROSS-EXAMINATION E

/ Els / anguish shoved between that spade and rock

we trenched ourselves against / əˈlo̅o̅mənəm /

that cubic foot in every possibility of saying / no̅ /

in four or five separate languages.

Else in our knowing, what would dig
might call her body curving to this trifold pick.

/ Els / in our grief we learned to use that word in other sentences

as / no̅ / meant little to / ə / ˈkəntrē / when its men had come to bury us.

Else knowing who would disappear
declared a wider rock.

/ Els / wider than each arm which carried us

to restitution clacking to that fourth spade

taking turns over / ə / ˈbädē / furthermore

how could you stand there and say nothing?

EXHIBIT E

E-tools excavated by that verb—*you stood there*
and said nothing—for entrenchment, to acknowledge
browning by our root. I wanted you to notice—
clanging downhill then another—snapped each
collarbone in two, that skeletal reminder by a surface.

No one spoke. No one saw this, in its speaking, but
You stood there and said nothing. How could I then
carry you, mama; or grow from underneath that tree;
or, after all, I wanted you to tell me, but you never
told me—*how did you escape them?*—by a shovel.

TESTIMONY F ["FIVE ASSUMPTIONS"]

MODERATOR: Can you tell us—

Yes, most of us were young and marked for what the body could or could not do, to clear this path against our nature; thus, to move we documented in each file:

"Meet the F-4 Phantom"

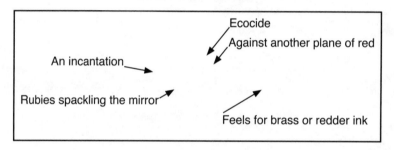

[Stamp: "Declassified"]

After this, I recognized you, sister, though the outline of your body faded in its microfilm. You wrote the word. I wrote, *Insurgency*, before the phantom blotting out a sulfurous white firmament stood by saying nothing.

CROSS-EXAMINATION (F.1)

/ ˈFīn(ə)lē / surrendering to distance

chalk lines kept a light on

feigning neither what would break / ə / monk

on / ˈfī(ə)r / smiling upon this figure of his body.

Fugue: how lately we run flying
on the left side of our flowers—

Lineage of salt ditched / ˈterəblē / of fathers

give or take / ə / fyoō / we lost to scraping

metallurgy in our mouths or just a few

surrendering by distance
then unfolding with a diagram of planes.

To hold this arm aloft, to call forth every wing—

and every wing could tumble after that—

You laid yourself on fire,
comrade, standing but said nothing.

EXHIBIT F

This was yours
in other words
a line and hook
between this fall-
out pattern

leading to its fold
this phantom-
thick parabola
an execution elsewhere

swooping in one arc
fallopian and swift
those sparrows
disappearing
down a pothole

then what flitted out
allegedly on fire thus
a ruby heart preserved.

CROSS-EXAMINATION (F.2)

Furthermore / əˈfär / the cupcake

topped with sugary blue blossoms

at a charitable bake sale in the U.S.

It was / ˈôfəl / said the pastor

simply / ˈôfəl / and we smiled

/ po͞ot / that cupcake down our shirt

and felt its icing coat our / ˈbelē /

in our minds / ə / blighted field

of fortitude would claw its way

from / ˈôfəl / holes / ə / blighted

sacred / härt / still beating.

CROSS-EXAMINATION (F.3)

After all we meant to / dī / but would not / dī / in their defense

our fathers covered up our faces when each soldier came

/ ə / fullness planking through our lines or fixed point turning—

On this axis, how we saw
a language of its absence
widening—

that sparrow flew into her throat.

TESTIMONY G ["GREASE WORK"]

MODERATOR: Can you tell us—

Yes. A grease work glowed, and we were nightly diagrammed: vestibules of ash upon its brick, the underlay of toil, dislocating gall with gladiolus, snapping at the instep built to hammer humanoid-machine; but you were there. I stood there and said nothing.

EXHIBIT G

Grease guns lent our spectacle
the image of what happened next
not why this happened or accounting
for its citizenry of hands disjointed
in between us, working by this pump
another way of saying, *Grip, Man!*
Have a grip, Man!—testimonies
taken, as they say, *Right off the hook.*

Two unlit grins, their statements—
no one ordered that, so no one went
to trial—but the girls unmanned
beside a text or darker grade of oil
made into this witness. You were
how we screamed back, sister, though
you never went to trial. Let us go.

SUPPLEMENTAL DIAGRAMS

All references to the incident stated previously (see *Exhibit G* and *Diagrams G-1* and *G-4*) are listed below, in their elemental order.

Note

This summary lists only those in question
Which directly affect the machine, *Exhibit G.*

Technical Order	Function	Lubricating Element
G-1	Nozzle	By the hose, we left a body Where her tonsils would have been
G-2	Armor Plating	A platelet billowed out *Or something like this, sir*
G-3	Oil Pressure	And pushing through skin-membrane Truly or effectively aglow That spirit separating from our bodies Therefore went to trial
G-4	Variable Duct Ramp	Gleaming capability, we left one standing Too
G-5	Cartridge	Dark nebulously You woke then I woke up
G-6	Transfer Gear	Was then filmed or made to bark
G-7	Afterburner Fuel	Just like a dog How could you stand there And say nothing

EXHIBIT (G.2)

Or the greater spirit punctured
diagrams of grease and marrow,

a threadfin's oaken
metallurgical production

that I, gaunt with petrol, made
this reportage and then in your dying,

sister, reborn a stag. I grappled
with a usage of a body

crying out,
so look up, ma.

I stand here, in your next life
transfigured by its form:

this fallen oak or galloping device
to dream of stags again

to bracket off the engine, one by
one to bring us back to trial.

TESTIMONY H ["HOW HUMAN OF HER"]

MODERATOR: Can you tell us—

Yes, how human of us noticing the helicopter pilot who had over-looked the target—follicle then scalp or hospital in ruins or an hour right before us honing into copper—who had ordered him to carry out this operation? Furthermore, you broke into my heart, comrade, a grafted face with every grafted hamlet, thus, a body in enactment broke my heart. I had no choice. You had no choice, beloved. Why did you just stand there and say nothing?

H.A.L.O. JUMP

Objective: think of harvest
Huey overhead or Howitzer

        this honeyed heartland
        bending to his sickle.

Pas de deux: the spine of which
made sweet two hieroglyphic

        gunshots following the gun-
        ner's weaponry of air.

Or who else was there? *Low
Opening*, his jump, the military

        shaken into haloes
        armed with—in the middle

red as marrow—holding
textures up against a dawn.

        I switched that light with
        something, less so, human.

You were human, comrade
taking shape: an offering

        sepia brown or hardening
        its glow upon inheritance.

I prayed to you or thought
bà ngoại, to pray despite

our vigilance, to launch
this hour's broken acronym:

H.A.L.O. or *to hide*,
Bà ngoại or harvests

far beneath us. And you
stood there but said nothing.

TESTIMONY I ["TEN OR FIFTEEN INCIDENTS"]

MODERATOR: Can you tell us—

Yes, [Redacted].

Note

Removal of this testimony was approved by
Headquarters, Department of the Army.

Please see *Figures I-1* through *I-10* for further
Investigation.

Americal Division, 198 LIB

Witness:

Was I better off alone, this historical adverb, shred of green?

The incident

An instance of each district
Dashed upon these faces of my makers

Tell me, sir, how was I equal?

[Stamp: "Declassified"]

SHORT RECESS

We've traveled far to say

    How this was brave
    If not unjust

The metal recess like a limit

    Justice dark as wind
    Whipped starlit dunes

Our juries whispered

    Reaching forward in
    Deliberation like an after-

Math of crimes ingrained

    To sentencing for
    What would happened

In that country of our people

    Made invasive withal
    Ordering this genocide

You were made a lie

    Inside of us, beloved
    How could I redact you?

TESTIMONY J ["JUST SORT OF REACHED OUT AND RETREATED"]

MODERATOR: Can you tell us—

At the hospital I reached out and retreated. From our word for *loss*, a word for *we*, and out of that, retreated, I was multiple and multi- all at once, each testimony lingering with signage. Yes, this really happened. I was there. You stood there but said nothing.

TESTIMONY K ["SPREAD-EAGLE"]

MODERATOR: Can you tell us—

Yes, there was a key in the doubling of knees, persimmon red; this conjunctive article, somewhere in the dialect buried deep inside each and every one of us, or how could you know what happened without her confession? I held my tongue, and then holding it out, I barked like a dog on film. How could you stand there, comrade?

CROSS-EXAMINATION (K.1)

Known: all kinds of backsliding on

/ ˈRekərd / let these records show / rəˈkôrdiNG /

Means by which we kept our bones uncovered.

CROSS-EXAMINATION (K.2)

Re: "re-"

          / rə'   kəv(ə)rē

          / *relentlessly*

                     / *that opening*

          / spred / 'ēgəl

          / ˌemblə'madik / əv / *excision, I recall*

          / *that symbol of my face which, opened, looking back*

          / *requested water.*

AKA   What pacified our protest flicking on then off
                     that bulbous heart

          Those other ways of speaking

AKA   Of / 'rekərds / with no end

          That punctuated, nullifying keel, that closing off
                     of brackets bending

          This way and then that

          No circumstantial evidence

          What pacified according to our terms,
                     we gave that / ˌôdə'madik / word
                     its automatic end.

EXHIBIT (K.1)

Toward this room a stag returned an infinite caesura bore us kin

EXHIBIT (K.2)

K.2.A.   *Hillside*

Dashing wordlessly forward, a spectral
reenactment in that place I counted down
to halting knee-deep at the summit—

K.2.B.   *Silvergrass*

A green unlettered bush—*miscanthus*—
crimes of carbon uphill; here at least
a shadow-beastly tale inside our field.

K.2.C.   *Martial Law*

I ran my hand, a vast and bitter knowing
on a clavicle, and who was slaughtered,
sister? There's no word outside of that

enacted like a prism at the Volta
for our highland bled out year by year,
and how could we survive its memory?

TESTIMONY L ["GOOD LAUGH FROM THAT—"]

MODERATOR: Can you tell us—

Lest we flood, lest currents roaring out of us,
resound becoming animal or animal

        of tongue, that impasse made impossible

that remnant of its wound. In other words,
who rose up, phoenix by her lacerating

        tone, bell by its bell, tolling our final laugh.

Who, soldiered, had this laugh? What blazing
through her bush became that Volta, dear

        lieutenant? Did you speak, becoming voice

that sinkable red sorrow? Làm sao, I spoke
back between us, broken statements in two

        parts. Believe me then. What leapt into

that body, killed her better engine. Lest
what followed made its truth by marginal

        assumption sinking through. I stood.

I stood again, each shadow-duplicating noun,
that, I as we, rendered perspective, two by

        tongue, that testified, becoming crash.

I crashed into you, colonel. Don't you know?
I laughed then laughed in Volta, then our

        ore-black inkwell spilling over. Look into

what rose, what lifting up her neck, arrived
another myth, once, what by fodder

                    cannon, infantry, admiral, died by you,

my colonel. Look, what winter phoenix
gazing up, became that other question—

                    làm sao, why did you just stand there?

ALLEGATIONS

MARGINS, AFFIRMATIONS

May that father enter shape then form, at last

Made marginal by force. May he affirm what crime

Marking his chest—a flag, that lash of welted ring,

That fractured verb or sternum indicating what

Once hooked then dragged behind his plow—thus

Wrote our similes for peace: red as his war, young

As his boys who butchered us. If only that may

Fall, our shape made marred by soldered oath

His laws that nation swore by: first, dropped into

Jungles; then, pronouncing dead, our beastly forms

Made red then winged. I rose from that unharmed.

I rose, for I was timed as brown among his other

Treatise. May that poem make, for us, this amulet

Of justice. May that enter shape then lore, my love

Fighting to live, so one day we might meet you.

MISE-EN-SCÈNE

Congressionally, I was set ajar—the structured room, an inquiry's disarmament—
and you were there. The subcommittee watched. The winter pine bent under wind.

And winter soldiers dreamt our fathers woke inside his country sent to trial. *Mise-en-scène*: I barked then stamped my foot onstage. You took our photograph which

pivoted its missive filled with monographs of war—a copy of the room, a copy
of the dog, allegedly defenseless, made to crawl around the country of your killers

—ma. I did exactly what they needed me to do and then survived because of that—
I barked out like a dog. Who else stood by, the dog and then the stag; yes, I was both.

AMULETS OF M

3:24 A.M.   I could not camp.

               You spoke into this being
                   Mournfully decolonized

               Our miniature tree.

3:26 A.M.   Making American domestic
                   Amulets of green.

3:46 A.M.   In place of plains misplacing
                   Genocidal mouths becoming

               Earth, our miniature noun.

3:43 A.M.   Làm sao, where you raked.

               Wherefore memorial of camps
                   Twinkled inside, I could recall

               You named us there, that guava seed.

3:56 A.M.   Made green once more, American

               Domestic.

4:26 A.M.

4:46 A.M.   Made
                        Before, was Vietnamese

                   Misplacing for my daughter.

4:46 A.M.   Why did you not wait?

4:36 A.M.   Twinkling
                        Amulet of love

                   I understood you then.

4:44 A.M.   And bent, làm sao, whispering, *how?*

                   That amulet upholding,
                        You'd care for me this way.

                   Undone, or timeless tree.

3:24 A.M. Undone, timelessly warred,
            I'd pen another spine. Therefore

            What staggers forward makes a stag.

            Whispering, *how?*

3:34 A.M. That drips into us, hoofs.

3:34 A.M. Why did you wait?
            Why do you wait, my love?

TESTIMONY N ["NASCENT NUDE RECLINING UNDER MOONLIGHT . . ."]

Nascent nude reclining under moonlight: Thorns embedded where they shouldn't be

The *mise-en-scène*:   A monument in dashing forward in procession for misnaming

What was left or who was left still nude: That woman by her river and these beetles

Flown in two directions: Truncating these glassy wings instead of that: A minute

Under moonlight: You were there, too, comrade. But you stood there and said nothing.

EXHIBIT (N.1)

Nebulae of static impositions—

Wait, that rocking dark of night
Regaining traction where we shouldn't be.

Rocking to front,
Rocking to back away—

That gated cap—

That graveled
Wood of history.

Yes, for example—
Broken in memory.

Tết Offensive, what might cause our heart

Lips brought
To ignition
Wiping out—

Closer inspection, how that jungle
Overtook its harvest—

Closer—

That was made
In self-defense.

Naming—

Yes, rabid, my eyes. Naming
Black opal for these eyes.

AMULETS OF N

Knave of steel: I made the labyrinth from tonus

Or my country from impossible desires, not that you were wounded

Loping through this outer wall made bestial by law

Instead of breath, the crosshair's light beholden to amaze us

Thus you spoke through me: a behemoth of power with no power,
Nhà for home, or Lúc Nhá Nhem for what might cross

Each marginal detachment, thus I armed, beloved, with a heart

And with that heart: you made a cry for justice.

N, OR VARIATIONS OF HAIBUN

I.

Hills of lemongrass and eucalyptus, neither here nor there, I sensed them long before two fighter jets roamed couplets overhead: a merciless enactment, gentle under fire—what was nullified, my country or another way of speaking.

"A" for "Anthem" boomed
from one hill to these valleys
tattered army flags.

II.

In Vietnamese, our word for *verse* is *thi*; and *sister*—notice how, in slanting both, a diacritic mark below these letters, *i* and *ị*—were also known as *thị*; these words for "thu" meant, without slanting, *that which fell after my sorrow*; "thùy," *to hang upon and dry*, these greener sides of time. Then all was silent in your language, and my language, as an elephant emerged out of the thicket.

Sorrowful trunks swayed
back and forth, the elephants
without their baby.

III.

Sunlight: mourning trumpets, elephants around the tiniest of bodies. Yes, I saw them. They would gather, one by one, along the river Mekong. Who eventually emerged and gestured with her bloody arms, a mythic queen without her head, who called out, *Comrade.*

Sisters, Hai Bà Trưng
declared their rebel forces
girls of document.

IV.

Silkworms screaming, tense with white mulberry leaves—arriving here, I wondered: who or what trampled that warfare into beast or man? Calico-green ammunition lined my memories like this from 1883 to 1945, therefore rendering me singular, or, neither here nor there. Another season passed and, later, strange four-legged ghosts.

Dyed a ylang-ylang green,
the beating moth-cocoon made
moths of us, unmanned.

EXHIBIT (N.2)

Saddled elephants with bells—
     a legendary trumpet
charging into marsh
   a helm of green; two sisters

born up north, a stratagem
     martially weakened
over clay; to cut off
   both her breasts, allegedly

one sister led her sister,
     both atop their elephants
leading a people
   once again, against invasion—

art surrendered to no one
     but a dynasty of queens.
I asked you, comrade,
   what happened then in 43 AD?

To paint her teeth a lacquer
     black, Sơn mài instead
of conquer neither beastly
   nor heroic; to be a sister first

citizen last, I stood there
     and said nothing.

TESTIMONY O ["SOME SORT OF AN ORIFICE"]

Operating as a function of what took her stand, I wrote the sil-
houette as ours, a testifying orifice refracting through prisms
then a vow you could never wash off though you tried, and

one, who signed with her palms: there was red everywhere,
photographs of a body dancing on the wall; this was alle-
gory for a country without sparrows. At night you witnessed,

too, the oracle making knots from a ritual wrapping itself
thrice around a hunting knife, words made wordless; too, this
was not supposed to happen, though it happened every day.

You saw the footage then its proof, a double-faced machine
blinking—*O* by *O*—as though to admit breath in her sound
of a shape flying through the shadow I was homed like this.

OTTAVA RIMA ENDING WITHOUT O

I.

There were people facing trial. Winter

Soldiers' photographic distance, mangrove

Over Mê Kông reddening its borders

Between document and justice. One drove

To this hammer, crying down then splintered

Off from nails and grain against a deep clove

Brown; that counterpart, our soldier's thralldom;

We were therefore peopled without freedom.

II.

Thus we shouted, *O*—each firebombing
        route to walk upon or set ablaze;

Each hospital reportedly abandoned
        justifying confidential crimes

Inside their confidential war; each raw-
        hide tanning gurneys speaking

Otherwise; each following an *O*—
            each shattering mistaken for

These other ways to implement a poem
            into action. What could justify

You, ma? I stood there but said nothing.

AMULETS OF O

Central to Đà Nẵng
uncovered hundred faces
switched up nouns.

I couldn't write. Or 1968
I couldn't speak. What part
of me was shocked? There-

fore an orifice deceived;
and I was razed to jumble
pyrophoric kinks

ferocious as our compound
partially declassified as tan.
The amulet, a sentence

without limbs. I couldn't
walk out from such frames
unharmed; and you were

there but saying nothing,
comrade. I was just a girl.
And you were just a girl.

O-GRAFT

Operating as a gesture for containment:
     tongue and serpentine, exceptionally placed.
   I opened up my home. The article, a dash instead
       of *O—*   A girl was shot uphill. Her gesturing

My light. That much I knew of operational
     intelligence, the centralizing articles for love.
   You walked into my home. You drank up all my water
     and two months over the spout. I ran out of my home

This human zone for reason. Meanwhile
     someone hunted someone else, and someone
  called that archival, the combing of my hair with saffron
      gesturing endurance, for my name you wrote in petrol

Vietnamese: *Detritus, O—*   *Divine.*
   I witnessed sentences by breath, and you
  had cried out, *Sister, O—*   *We did not want this.*
     That was known: this quadrangle of nouns, a graft

Over my skin made lighter than the color.
    Over that, a mouth; and under that, a human
  heart with antlers.

EXHIBIT O

Operating as our gesture,
               Lady Quan Âm glanced

Into that function of her throne,
               A merciful conjunction,

Light becoming wren,
               Whatever flew out bulged

Ten thousand acres scorching
               Milliseconds; sixty

Thousand girls who made
               From steel our terror,

Multiplied, ablaze;
               Quan Âm who spoke,

You did not want this. O—
               we do not want this.

TESTIMONY OF THE PLEIADES

Glimmered down
a reassembling of parts

that overnight conjunction
start there, *you said,*

Comrade, grass of teak
made crucible each word

our basis of retelling
sheet by sheet, too white.

Sky's indigo unbroken,
you said, constellated.

We were wronged then
counted proximal

by cluster. We were
nearby, infiltrated,

you said, enemy of state
—*what could not be*

tribunal—you said,
pointing up to heaven.

CLUSTER P, OR SEVEN AMULETS

I. Maia, or that elder of us—

       Ruptured
Hundred million pieces
                  You extracted

       Caulking up our staircase
          Colt-black metal eyelets
  We announced in sparring

II. Mảnh đạn, coded for Electra—

   Propagated   Reckless one of amber
She who lost in sundering
                      Civilian of Troy
             That largesse made
      Immobile

III. Halcyon of Taygete—

  You mistook her for a comet
           That in knowing blurred
     Its pallid mark

          A dash of green by seascape
Roving tridents glinted

IV. Alcyone—

                                                                She who therefore swore
        Or purposeful glissando
Eyes then curving out
Resounding to

                Some dictionary term
        For what once   Generously thrown   Sown into constellation

V. Spoken by Celaeno—

        We were mothered   In accordance   Hatching from that tree
                                        A kumquat
                        And apart
                A coral   You were tendered   (Yes)

Red hatchets from the ground

VI. Asterope—

                Clustered parallax   Our contact ground's munitions
Who was promptly thrown

                        Its antipersonnel
                                Who smote that sky
                                Made seven of us

                Formally above   (Demilitarized)

VII. Song of Merope—

        You then prompted—*I could stand there and say nothing*—dropped

What followed
Pointed into night   Or smattering of shells—*I call that vision*

TESTIMONY Q ["[REDACTED] AS THE QUALITY"]

"And as the quality of Vietnamese love differs from ours,
so does the nature of their hate."

(Susan Sontag, *Trip to Hanoi*)

[Redacted] as the quality of loosening by wire,
    dirge by nation, yes, in spite of that

dethroned, I penned another—*noun by operative*
    function yanking from your hand—

Or loving back [redacted], excavated, what was
    patterned? You can't know for sure.

Comrade, every week of watching whittled for
    [redacted], what was functional

—*alloy, red copper, or [redacted]*—charging,
    blown into three pieces. Yes,

I counted. First, you stood there—*as the quality*
    [redacted]—differed from your nature,

I was sound and soundless, neutralized by query
    —*how did you [redacted]?*—

I was lettered, *Q* by spark, [redacted]. Second,
    I was kumquat for QUEBEC, a caliber

machine, thus you were loaded; third, [redacted]
    for its operative killing. My beloved,

as the quality of justice differs from your nature,
  so does qualifying nature of [redacted].

Write that down—*a spectacle of trial*—in which,
  falling sound and soundlessly [redacted].

TESTIMONY R ["ROUNDED UP"]

Rounded up by gender
Stories of our leaving

                           Have their wattage, child

At the back end I left you a clustering of copper

                    Amulets spackled without their mirrors

You were spinning courtside
Oath by occupation

                       You were laughing, child

Woven into tapestries of gold
Or village where

               My mother left you hidden

Once again we raised ourselves among each child

               Of our killers, ma, what wept

Behind us in that bassinet of mulberry
Or rounding

                    Up, we multiplied like birds.

REDACTIONS FROM AN INTERNATIONAL
WAR CRIMES TRIBUNAL

1.   *Has the Government [redacted] for aggression?*
      Yes (conclusively).

2.   *What was reestablished by this action?*
      You were all I wanted.

3.   *If found guilty of complicity [redacted], would you—*
      Yes.

4.   *Have the Governments of the United States, [redacted], and [redacted] been complicit to inhuman treatment of [redacted] population?*
      How could I misquote you?

5.   *Is the Government [redacted] guilty of [redacted]?*
      Comrade, please forgive me. You were all I wanted.

6.   *Have the armed forces of [redacted] utilized [redacted] weapons strictly prohibited by international law?*
      Yes (unanimously).

7.   *And if so, on what scale?*
      I learned orthographic letters—*R* pronounced as *Zed*—[redacted]. Whether your intention was [redacted], could you name me after trial? Somehow I chose to protect that in a poem. How could I misread you—*R* for *radium [redacted]*, *ROK*, or *recon*—I was learning, but you could not name me.

8.   *Have prisoners of war [redacted] by the armed forces of [redacted] been subjected to mistreatment by international law?*
      Yes.

9.   *Have the [redacted]—*
      Yes (conclusively).

10.   *And if so, on what scale, [redacted] for example, hospitals, [redacted], medical [redacted], monuments, etc.?*
      Comrade, you were found repeatedly misquoted. I was faulty, calling you when I was weakest. Therefore, you were wanted.

11.   *Is the Government of Japan guilty of [redacted] [redacted] by the Government of the United States against Vietnam?*
      Yes (unanimously), after all, he was my father. You knew, too. Is that why you could hold me?

12.   *Are the Governments of Australia, New Zealand, and [redacted], guilty of complicity in the [redacted] by the Government [redacted] in Vietnam?*
      Comrade, you must know by now.

13.   *Have the armed [redacted] of the United States subjected the civilian [redacted]—*
      Yes. Why do you ask?

14.   *Who is guilty?*

15.   *Have forced labor camps [redacted]?*
      You were there. I saw you.

16.   *Has there been [redacted] of the population or [redacted] tending to [redacted] which can be [redacted] as [redacted] acts of genocide?*
      I felt you. How could you look back—pronouncing *Zed—O*, Priestess, please have mercy on our souls.

17.   *Cobra, red bird.*
      You were there. I saw you burning. You were all I wanted.

BYLAWS

BYLAW [S.1] STRING-AND-WIRE ABECEDARIAN

Stop. There is no cipher
Only sorrow. You must know
By now, Comrade—*A*.

Guided by Missile; B.
Sonar; Tactical Division—
Highlands into parts,

That centralizing zone,
I was there—*Irregular; On-*
Going Zone; D. En Route—Stop.

● ━ ━ ━

Stop. A poisoned river
Thus rerouted. Stop.

● ● ━ ━ ━

Stop. For any failed attempt
Meant fleeing—*Glossa; F. Mid-*
Highland—wired, then we—

Somewhere in a thicket
There were rabbits screaming. Stop.

● ● ● ━ ━

Stop. As you were wired, made into a game
—*J. Killed in Action*—justifying torture

Through this method—*Citizen in Question;*
Laughing Could Not Stop Her Laughing—Stop.

● ● ● ━

Stop. I wired—*Population*—subject to in-
Human treatment. Rabbits, coded—*No.*

You wired back—*O. Mechanized Platoons*
Equipped With Arms—who could believe me?

Regimented—R. Come Forward—Stop.

● ● ● ● ●

Stop. That is your sorrow.
You must know, comrade—*U.*

Unarmed; Civilian Expected
To Retreat—mistaken for—

V. Enemy in Shadow; Overrun—
Memory's displacement.

X. On Sight; Pronouncement; Y.
White Wood Line; Universal—Stop.

— • • •

Stop. That is my sorrow.
Stop. I could not stop you.

— — • • •

Zippo—ambush; wire—*Missions*—
Codifying—*silver; straw*—that difference
Made italicized then strung along a water.

Comrade, no, I could not stop you—*Z.*
That Broken Line Between Us.

BYLAW [S.2] NOTES FOR IMMEDIATE DISPATCH

J. Encoded   Subsequently

Photographed then sent abroad

Made evident encoding

That resistant   Brown

I bodied kilos   *K. Ladder*   Abecedarian which blossomed

L. Small Bowls of Rice

Immediately Dispatched

Acted without orders or reflection   *N. For Nước*

Or National Diplomacy

Grounds by which I found

Prohibited by law   *Q. For Tango*

Charlie—   *Delta, Delta—*

Made myself   *X. Tangled Up*

BYLAW [S.3] OBJECT LESSON

Amulet ● —

Charged by touch
A month [redacted], 1967 — ● ● ●

For its emphasis — ● — ● *Ore*

Uranium coded to blaze
I was smoked — ● ●

● In smoking out

That amulet quoted by no one
● ● — ● Flaring—*Belemnite*

Red Opal to Red Jasper

Elemental — — ● Airborne
Forced into its shape

Đắk Tô then split ● ● ● ●

A desecrated hill
One followed by another ● ●

    Murmured ● — — — *No*

An Amulet of Wind, An Amulet by Dust — ● —
● — ● ● That also in their braying

    Oxen — — Caught crossing

Astonished — ●
By their clang — — — You stood there

    Bò—friendly by fire ● — — ●

Stop — — ● — I called that verbiage
● — ● Shaped into a movement

    Upwardly ● ● ● Soaring in place

What you then made of us
What consequently — Shone

    Dear Bò, I crossed, too

Flesh into fur ● ● —
Đắk Tô, that other line between us

     ● ● ● — Battering each horn

Astounded by their use
● — — For you were there

     That amulet of bone — ● ● —

Named—*elemental, mythic*
— ● — — *beast by language* — — ● ●

     Both, an object for its keeping

SALMON	SSR-573
SEAWOLF	SS-197
FIFTEEN KNOTS	Ss

Saigon to Moscow

TANGO ["YES, I SAW IT HAPPEN THIRTY, FORTY TIMES"]

MODERATOR: Can you tell us—

I. Yes, I saw it happen thirty, forty times — Exterminated — — — Resting • — • Yesterday, I told the court — And now I'd like to add • • — [Redacted] • — • In all honesty, upon my mother's life • Nobody turned away.

II. That lesson for mistreatment — I was wrested from an order made executive by treatment — — — You were resting though nobody turned away • — • I told your court — I lied • • — For now I'd like to add that, in all honesty, we ran into a bush • — • Which made an awful sound • [Redacted], in all honesty, or something like this, sir.

III. And for your record, we were resting — I was resting, too — — — Though none of us could sleep after that year • — • I told your court as much — In Đà Nẵng • • — Then Aleppo • — • Thus nobody turned away • I went there for my mother.

IV. For tribunals had no reach beyond our century of dying.

V. I was placed — Misplaced with every record, made into our country — — — Yesterday, I told your court • — • *[Redacted], sir* — And we were martially decoded • • — In all honesty • — • [Redacted] • Though nobody looked away.

VI. Soldiers were recycled — Thus begot a rebel — — — You were running, sir, uphill • — • On Đồi A Bia, near Laos — I was dreamt up • • — Bestial then martial by the stones • — • Our separating place that Sarajevo woke • Our traumas ran into another.

VII. Thirty, forty times — My mother saw it happen in that city of her mother — — — But I could not count us, sir, to document it all ● — ● Honest truths of war — [Redacted] ● ● — Used outside tribunal ● — ● Every face made blank ● Nobody turned away.

VIII. For in the news, I saw a video recording.

IX. In that video recording — Men forcing a man to speak — — — Who blinked through every letter ● — ● Spoken in his meantime — *I'm okay* ● ● — *They feed me well* ● — ● [Redacted] ● *In all honesty, I miss my mother and my wife.*

X. For in our video recordings, I became the enemy of time.

XI. For in that state of lying — Men took precedential truths — — — To speak by law and universal laws ● — ● Recycled every word — *I was okay* ● ● — *They fed me well* ● — ● I told your court ● *[Redacted], sir.*

XII. Losing count of war crimes meant a war crime never happened. Therefore, I was tortured.

XIII. Yes, it happened thirty, forty times — Injustice made — — — [Redacted] ● — ● After thirty, forty times — I was okay ● ● — Then I was freed ● — ● In Sài Gòn made to ● In that city of my mother.

XIV. Thirty, forty times, a lesson in mistreatment — Who could testify that nothing ever happened, but this happened — — — You were looking ● — ● And I could not look away — That testifying, ran into a bush and made an awful sound ● ● — *[Redacted]* ● — ● Wife or mother ● In our state of dying.

XV. Uphill, in a country not my own, I found her body, sir.

XVI. From that body, I could write our book of testimonies. But I could not write this by myself.

XVII. Uphill, yes — I saw it happen thirty, forty times — — — Examples of mistreatment ● — ● Held in Nuremberg, in London — Up to trial ● ● — But I could not write it plainly ● — ● By myself ● Alone, that is therefore, a poem.

XVIII. I was tried — Or seen by trial — — — Made examples of mistreatment ● — ● Pinched into this ceremony — Justice ● ● — But I could, comrade ● — ● Not like that stag or grassland of his dreams ● I could not write just that.

XIX. But you were right — These poems showed us no more — — — Optimistic ● — ● You were done with testifying — What would never happen ● ● — Running ● — ● Uphill ● By myself.

XX. And you were coded — Universal — — — Or, in fact ● — ● Etc. — The outline of what never happened by confession ● ● — But I wrote that ● — ● And my spirit answered back ● Yes, you were there.

XXI. For the courtroom makes our barricade of creatures.

XXII. For the jury makes this bodied — But I saw it happen thirty, forty times — — — Our universal outline for some confidential crime ● — ● That tributary grid — [Redacted] ● ● — Came up as our engine ● — ● Up for trial ● Left upon exhibit.

XXIII. Speaking in the microphone, another man. Or witness, sir.

XXIV. Who could stand there but say nothing — I remembered, sir, the country — — — Standing on his table • — • For exhibit — Spectacle on hand • • — The universal soldier with a universal statement • — • Televised for Congress • You were silent.

XXV. I told you — Language broke our barricade of laws — — — [Redacted] • — • I was there — One blueprint for injustice in a matrix of injustice • • — Reenacted • — • Reprohibited • Enacted once again.

XXVI. Chemical amnesia — Redeveloped — — — Or those methods of destruction given to another • — • That is, that was, time — Blueprints pre[Redacted] • • — Precedential • — • Taken from Vietnam • Comrade, I reenacted.

XXVII. Somehow you misdialed, sir, the military template.

XXVIII. Recognizing of this pattern — Stared into those blinking eyes — — — Our crimes which never happened • — • But one happened, sir — Responsible for universal speaking • • — Sonar or • — • [Redacted] • For [Redacted].

XXIX. We're almost there.

XXX. We're almost at the verdict — Uphill — — — Recognized what happened to its template • — • Or the gridline — Meter after meter • • — Stinking of its ashes • — • Out of that, what soared • I reenacted, sir.

F-4 PHANTOM II   XF4H-1

937-METER BARRICADE   Rr

HILL 937   Crouching

Saigon to Belgrade

AUBADE BEFORE TRIBUNAL

Hill 937. Let me offer you from Sa Huỳnh
copper bowls and lingling-o, that double-headed
amulet of milky nephrite green. Our ceremony

calls for this. Now hold my spirit steady.
At its base, regard my grandmother—some one
thousand, seven hundred sixty-eight years later,

south of Đà Nẵng—coded daily with its embers.
Enemy of State or Enemy of Earth, who could
channel differentials, that which hunted people

like a nation in a nation? Let me offer us that
monumental sconce meaning: nobody heard you
burning, but I heard you burning, comrade.

Rise up. For that evidential dawn might shimmer
tempest red, our later modes of slaughter or address.
So let me rise up with you, comrade, shaking off

these golden embers from each wing. And let me
tell you of our people and our beastly creatures
walking with us—double-headed oxen and red

double-headed lions—resurrected with dark brass,
carnelian, and jade. I'll meet you there, upon a hill
inside a country, that which hunted years

into a ceremony, that which called us skyward
so one day I'd meet you, ma.

MORNING CEREMONY

ERDL PATTERN, CEREMONY U

[Redacted: *Umber*]

Note

Removal of this shade has been approved
By Headquarters, Department of the Army.

Please see Figures U-4 and U-8 for further
Uses of the color.

I. Tropical utility in predeveloped form, a leafy tan and brown, issued our bodies out.

II. In 1967, scholars organized a trial for your people. I was pallid. You recoiled like a rosebush
   testifying soil.

III. Blossomed, too, aberrant roses.

IV. Comrade, understand that some were slaughtered without trial. You were pallid. Let us start
   from pigment—*Umber*—sprouting from this soil.

V. Poplin by design, our uniform survived beyond its reason.

VI. F-4 Phantom Priestess, unarmed, you carried that verdict made of jasper.

VII. Understand this, sir, for when a riverboat explodes, I'll stand and just say nothing.

DICTUMS OG-107, CEREMONY V

[Addition: *Olive Green*]

Note

The testing of this shade has been approved
By Headquarters, Department of the Army.

Please see *Figures V-4* and *V-10* for further
Uses of the color.

I. I was channeled, spoken by that sunburst.

II. Vaulting through wide crevices of noun, our rooms were filled with music.

III. Only then described by reoccurrence, Jean-Paul Sartre wrote—*There Is No Question*—but our
spectacle of green. And you were channeled, too.

IV. To vocalize as such, to multiply, that which built up, shone among our bodies.

V. Voluminous and gossamer, I piled every flower on our altar.

VI. Red flowers then burned.

VII. In lying down, I glistened. Vestibules were parted, hungering like bushes. Then that sweetness
came and left.

VIII. That was our preservation, offering up prayers like a scent. I could not amplify.

IX. Adjacent then.

X. To varnish without drink, to drink without a cup, that water drank us slowly.

XI. Sparrows stuffed into this wall inside our empty room, though nothing more could shock
us after 1963.

XII. Then costumes changed. Each sparrow gripped a knife between their tiny beaks. An olive green
was varnished, clipped, subsumed just like our own.

XIII. Who stole away, lastly, each flower from our altar?

CEREMONY W ["SHE COULD HAVE DROWNED, SHE COULD HAVE SWAM UNDER WATER, SHE COULD HAVE GONE ANYWHERE."]

MODERATOR: Can you make that amulet of love?

Incident Report:

The swamp and mangrove, too
Withholding of her outcome, who was led

Across her bridge [Redacted]
Northern province

Motorized disunion jumping forward
Could be orderly

A suspect for mistreatment by your people, sir
That ceremony made, allegedly, its end

You stood right there
You stood and just said nothing

CEREMONY X, OR DOUBLE-HEADED STONES

How existing on that basis of retelling
We could excavate a letter   Martyred seamlessly

Example testifying, *Woman*
As our own collective spirit   *—A: Undoing Ambush*

—W: An Incidental SOP
That diacritic's gesturing lieutenant   No

We could not help him and Quan Âm
Those double-headed beasts   We stood then knelt

—X: Quadrant
Massed   Prohibited by form extenuating what crossed

Shaken from an altar but you stood there saying nothing.

CEREMONY Y, UNIVERSAL GRID

MODERATOR: Can you make that amulet of love?

1.   You ought to visit when monsoon is done, and all the cows have come down from sabbatical.

2.   We tied string around our necks to help you differentiate between last century and thirst. But you must know this has not hampered with our cooking.

3.   Cultivated May through summer, tiger lilies shrank from scythes.

4.   You've "seen it done to women," bitten at an ear and nose like leather satchels nailed above our rivers. Clattering inside a frame, you've seen it done to women.

5.   Yes, you ought to know we phoned when there was money.

6.   Flowing in receivers, varnish chirped from walls.

7.   You meant no harm. You yelped and shrank your hind legs like a dog. Weren't you that dog?

8.   We boosted signals, carried dolls, the physicality which countered any semblance of fear.

9.   Or giving evidence in clear, featureless manners we could not expect our faces for that matter rolling down what cracked into the jungle.

10. You remembered much of this back then.

11. You transferred claw marks for miasma like the excrement had dried.

12. Likewise some kept pictures posing next to us like sharks pulled out the ocean, hanging from our jaws.

13. You've threaded wires like good sports, old sport.

14.   Our yearning gritted rock beneath our fingernails.

15.   Caressing bark.

16.   In-grooves gutted our trees with water, nothing else; and yonder mapped perdition; yonder war symphonic bell tops glistened in the sun.

FINAL REPORT

MODERATOR: Can you make that amulet of love?

Before I realized that mirror held us up—

    a zephyr like the pyre
  throwing smoke into its wind
      turned us in every wrong direction
        though we trusted it.

    Why should I trust you now?

Zygotic marbles grieved
  a wounding hole thus yoked
    thus otherwise departing
          jagged like an etch
its oil, steel, and canisters
      cut-
    tagging like a zipper.

Zenith cried, for currencies
      were never floating then.

  To sanctify our zone, diaspora
Zirconia ink-
    hard zastruga, zinc
      crisscrossing over plains.

  A unison by ziggurat, that tortured
    by its half.

We mounted this
to verbal
zeppelin
that summing up zero parts in sum.

That zone an afterword
of zed by light purveying
zests of nearly wordless lighting.

See, comrade, an index broken up.

CLOSING STATEMENT

The woman, who is absent, sings inside her chamber. Look

She decorates a mirror. Citrine. Slabs of marbled agate-blue

And in this way, our wheel begins to turn the woman in her work.

Z   And as we've heard over the past five days, a gilded light
                                    departing stood for justice.

No one spoke within a court of law, reversible or found.

Wherein to tuck our testimonies subsequently falling
                                through that hill, our voices

Y   filled that room.

On-site, each sunken note was conscious—climbing, therefore,
                             parted—one before the other

clef with latitude, each form of measurement which measured
                             crimes of war using the other.

X   Thus we answered back our nation into action, action into bowls
                             zapping each wire into place

without each plastic in a bowl.

Yes, it was very clear what happened.

Upon that hill we held a crater with the rope and nail; reloading
W   once what was a blade

and sharpened pieces of white soap, as one began to speak

in place of hands

upon the mirror. Blue became the goat—con dê.

Con ong became the bee, a warm—đu đủ—papaya would then
ripen.

V

Yes, without a doubt, the woman split into our singing.

Sun measured that instance zipping up a wire which was placed
before our blast container.

In conclusion, wherefore cutting up the glass, we felt
around for blades.

U

Yes, it was very clear what happened on that hill.

A restoration paved the goat inflected by its phalanx by a policy
alone settling crimes;

and settlement yielded a bridge, in Hội An, for example.

T

In a year we would recall, clearly, what happened crossed
over the bridge

and read aloud a taxonomic growth—behavior knotting up
our cherry trees;

and what we needed was a stem to cut up all the wires
kneading at the goat,

S

the throat of it, our sacrifice.

To eat the bee, a xylophone imported from the highlands
                              trenched into a rock,

we matted formulas.

R

Our formulations counted every ribbon.

What we needed was a way out of the abscess, draining liquid
                              with its pressure.

Necessary, waning out the body, absently, we indicated yet
                              what wobbled down

Q

survived that hill in 1966.

That visible, as yet, that otherwise awake, quite happy now
                              to be alive; that dressed

her selves, and Panda, too, brushing his several teeth;
                              that dressed her selves,

P

and Panda, making up the bed; that sang, for yet, a lilac
                              for occasion; that much

visible, as yet, to know its iteration; woman, absent, indicated
                              order staggering up odysseys.

Wherefore a testimonial had caved our last desire, almost nothing
                              shone.

O

The marbled stone—

The varnish by its motor grease or volumes intergreasing—

How we felt a rolling near the surface—

N   Wherein how we took the alphabet as ours—solicitation
                                        back to songs of solace

rounding up the spirits wild and awoken,

    wizened by its thunder, sấm sét và mây, thus, withal but singing
                                  moving arm-in-arm

M   to exit clouds, a boneless place, a zone zigzagging toward
                                 that greater undertow.

To tremble, teaming hearts, voluminously yowled bursting
                                 from a butterfly, we tugged

at tinted sculptures up our hill, a xerographic print collapsing
                                 xylem.

L   Tissue grassed a yellow sun yanking up everything.

A yellow ray then waved its hollow arms, an ulcerated wood
                                 upon the catalogue of song.

Our dance would thrum beneath each circumstance.

K   We posed such ultimatums:

            i. We'd like to have the woman's body back
                          the one left on that hill.

            ii. We'd like a second look at lacerations where they roped
                          my ankles to the wall.

J   *iii. I'd like another vowel, please.*

Or terracing the form, or otherwise, her marginality of error, yes,
                               we'd like my sandals, too.

And afterward, our freedom came to hold a price.

The joyful shift in key; that verified divide and wondrous—

I   I, between that vast collective, umber clamped upon my legs
                                  then pelvic bone; then quietly

between her screams.

We wrote the record of our trial, promised mercy.

H   Running bled utmost respectability for whom, we asked.

For who could free us then?

And stop the burning of our homes?

And follow horror to the end of time?

G   And feign each purple heart to crystallize?

And martial law, uranium?

Even that hill, that room of marching cities felt vibrations
                                puckering up grounds of—

Rattled gods awake.

F

That godless liberation—

    i. Liberate us, sister. Liberate us in our static.

    ii. Did you see the tank? And did you see our infants?
                    They were thrown!

E   *iii. And thrown beneath my body, I was torn.*

And parsing out the truth, an element of bone torn yawning
                     of our days, for we have

dreamt so desperately of a love for, more or less, one thousand
                     and four hundred years,

D   the magnitude toward which shadowed our masters into bone.

And finally, what did you make from all our billion faces
                     smiling in my orifice?

What did you dig from me? And what was written for a soldier?

Soldier, face me.

C

Did you not think that your daughters and the daughters
                     of your daughters

would dare tremble? Hanging from our lips? Before our lips?

Our lips revealing fangs?

B   And from this fang, did you not then begin to feel your sons?

        How do your sons inhabit apathy today?

        For you, alive, my killer—

        Sister—millions of faces in my faces—no, remember we have
                                  colored every memory

A

        from this, from which your children, ten-ten folding.

        Yes, for we must live squaring our faces through the wool-stitched
                                  fabric of our days;

        for we must send our bodies back.

        Remember what was done to us now moves through you
                                  whether you weep or not.

        Remember what was done to us commands no force
                                  beyond these trials laid out

        in this book.

        What one would therefore stab into our grounds, an odyssey
                                in flames, that wretched scent

        of petrol offering this statement like a torch.

        Kneeling, then I stood. Standing behind me, men would kneel.

        Together near our stag tumbling down that hill became a bird.

That hill then bird would stand behind me—warm
                                      beloved, near our sun.

I woke, mama, and smiled.

WINTER PHOENIX

ACKNOWLEDGMENTS

To the spirits who knocked against my heart, this book is your work and testimony. May you find rest, and may you leave this world in peace.

Poems from *Winter Phoenix* have been published in the following journals:

AAWW	Testimony A ["Absolutely Virtuous"]
	"Cross-Examination (A.1)"
	"Exhibit (A.1)"
Birdcoat Quarterly	"Bylaw [S.1] String-and-Wire Abecedarian"
The Cincinnati Review	"O-Graft"
	"Amulets of O"
Hayden's Ferry Review	Testimony R ["Rounded Up"]
	TANGO ["Yes, I Saw It Happen Thirty, Forty Times"]
The Iowa Review	"Expatriated Fugue"
New Delta Review	"Closing Statement"
Poetry Online	"Bylaw [S.3] Object Lesson"
Qu Literary Magazine	"Aubade before Tribunal"
	"Dictums OG-107, Ceremony V"
Salt Hill Journal	"18 November 1966"
	"19 November 1966"

Sundog Lit	Testimony Q ["[Redacted] as the Quality"]
	"Redactions from an International War Crimes Tribunal"
The Seattle Review	[from *Hill* 192] "We are ready to let the testimony say it all."
Tahoma Literary Review	"Margins, Affirmations"

ABOUT THE AUTHOR

Sophia Terazawa is the author of two chapbooks, *I AM NOT A WAR* (Essay Press), a winner of the 2015 Essay Press Digital Chapbook Contest, and *Correspondent Medley* (Factory Hollow Press), winner of the 2018 Tomaž Šalamun Prize. Her work has been published widely in journals and magazines, such as, *The Offing*, *New Delta Review*, *The Iowa Review*, and *The Rumpus*. She holds an MFA from the University of Arizona, where she served as poetry editor for *Sonora Review*. Her favorite color is purple, and she's managed by a tiny panda named Panda.

DONORS

Thank you all for your support.
We do this for you, and could not do it without you.

AVAILABLE NOW FROM DEEP VELLUM

Michèle Audin · *One Hundred Twenty-One Days* · translated by Christiana Hills · FRANCE

Bae Suah · *Recitation* · translated by Deborah Smith · SOUTH KOREA

Mario Bellatin · *Mrs. Murakami's Garden* · translated by Heather Cleary · MEXICO

Eduardo Berti · *The Imagined Land* · translated by Charlotte Coombe · ARGENTINA

Carmen Boullosa · *Texas: The Great Theft* · *Before* · *Heavens on Earth* · translated by Samantha Schnee, Peter Bush, Shelby Vincent · MEXICO

Magda Cârneci · *FEM* · translated by Sean Cotter · ROMANIA

Mathilde Walter Clark · *Lone Star* · translated by Martin Aitken and K. E. Semmel · DENMARK

Leila S. Chudori · *Home* · translated by John H. McGlynn · INDONESIA

Sarah Cleave, ed. · *Banthology: Stories from Banned Nations* · IRAN, IRAQ, LIBYA, SOMALIA, SUDAN, SYRIA & YEMEN

Ananda Devi · *Eve Out of Her Ruins* · translated by Jeffrey Zuckerman · MAURITIUS

Peter Dimock · *Daybook from Sheep Meadow* · USA

Claudia Ulloa Donoso · *Little Bird* · translated by Lily Meyer · PERU/NORWAY

Ross Farrar · *Ross Sings Cheree & the Animated Dark: Poems* · USA

Alisa Ganieva · *Bride and Groom* · *The Mountain and the Wall* · translated by Carol Apollonio · RUSSIA

Anne Garréta · *Sphinx* · *Not One Day* · *In Concrete* · translated by Emma Ramadan · FRANCE

Jón Gnarr · *The Indian* · *The Pirate* · *The Outlaw* · translated by Lytton Smith · ICELAND

Goethe · *The Golden Goblet: Selected Poems* · *Faust, Part One* · translated by Zsuzsanna Ozsváth and Frederick Turner · GERMANY

Noemi Jaffe · *What are the Blind Men Dreaming?* · translated by Julia Sanches & Ellen Elias-Bursac · BRAZIL

Claudia Salazar Jiménez · *Blood of the Dawn* · translated by Elizabeth Bryer · PERU

Jung Young Moon · *Seven Samurai Swept Away in a River* · *Vaseline Buddha* · translated by Yewon Jung · SOUTH KOREA

Kim Yideum · *Blood Sisters* · translated by Ji yoon Lee · SOUTH KOREA

Josefine Klougart · *Of Darkness* · translated by Martin Aitken · DENMARK

Yanick Lahens · *Moonbath* · translated by Emily Gogolak · HAITI

Fouad Laroui · *The Curious Case of Dassoukine's Trousers* · translated by Emma Ramadan · MOROCCO

Fernanda Garcia Lau · *Out of the Cage* · translated by Will Vanderhyden · ARGENTINA

Maria Gabriela Llansol · *The Geography of Rebels Trilogy: The Book of Communities*; *The Remaining Life*; *In the House of July & August* · translated by Audrey Young · PORTUGAL

Pablo Martín Sánchez · *The Anarchist Who Shared My Name* · translated by Jeff Diteman · SPAIN

Dorota Masłowska · *Honey, I Killed the Cats* · translated by Benjamin Paloff · POLAND

Brice Matthieussent · *Revenge of the Translator* · translated by Emma Ramadan · FRANCE

Lina Meruane · *Seeing Red* · translated by Megan McDowell · CHILE

Valérie Mréjen · *Black Forest* · translated by Katie Shireen Assef · FRANCE

Fiston Mwanza Mujila · *Tram 83*, translated by Roland Glasser · *The River in the Belly*, translated by J. Bret Maney · DEMOCRATIC REPUBLIC OF CONGO

Goran Petrović · *At the Lucky Hand, aka The Sixty-Nine Drawers* · translated by Peter Agnone · SERBIA

Ilja Leonard Pfeijffer · *La Superba* · translated by Michele Hutchison · NETHERLANDS

Ricardo Piglia · *Target in the Night* · translated by Sergio Waisman · ARGENTINA

Sergio Pitol · *The Art of Flight* · *The Journey* · *The Magician of Vienna* · *Mephisto's Waltz: Selected Short Stories* · translated by George Henson · MEXICO

Julie Poole · *Bright Specimen: Poems from the Texas Herbarium* · USA

Eduardo Rabasa · *A Zero-Sum Game* · translated by Christina MacSweeney · MEXICO

Zahia Rahmani · *"Muslim": A Novel* · translated by Matthew Reeck · FRANCE/ALGERIA

Juan Rulfo · *The Golden Cockerel & Other Writings* · translated by Douglas J. Weatherford · MEXICO

Oleg Sentsov · *Life Went On Anyway* · translated by Uilleam Blacker · UKRAINE

Mikhail Shishkin · *Calligraphy Lesson: The Collected Stories* · translated by Marian Schwartz, Leo Shtutin, Mariya Bashkatova, Sylvia Maizell · RUSSIA

Ófeigur Sigurðsson · *Öræfi: The Wasteland* · translated by Lytton Smith · ICELAND

Mustafa Stitou · *Two Half Faces* · translated by David Colmer · NETHERLANDS

FORTHCOMING FROM DEEP VELLUM

Shane Anderson · *After the Oracle* · USA

Mario Bellatin · *Beauty Salon* · translated by David Shook · MEXICO

Mircea Cărtărescu · *Solenoid* · translated by Sean Cotter · ROMANIA

Logen Cure · *Welcome to Midland: Poems* · USA

Leylâ Erbil · *A Strange Woman* · translated by Nermin Menemencioˇglu · TURKEY

Radna Fabias · *Habitus* · translated by David Colmer · NETHERLANDS

Sara Goudarzi · *The Almond in the Apricot* · USA

Song Lin · *The Gleaner Song* · translated by Dong Li · CHINA

Jung Young Moon · *Arriving in a Thick Fog* · translated by Mah Eunji and Jeffrey Karvonen · SOUTH KOREA

Fiston Mwanza Mujila · *The Villain's Dance* · translated by Roland Glasser · DEMOCRATIC REPUBLIC OF CONGO

Johnathan Norton · *Penny Candy* · USA

Ludmilla Petrushevskaya · *Kidnapped: A Crime Story*, translated by Marian Schwartz · *The New Adventures of Helen: Magical Tales*, translated by Jane Bugaeva · RUSSIA

Sergio Pitol · *The Love Parade* · translated by G. B. Henson · MEXICO

Manon Stefan Ros · *The Blue Book of Nebo* · WALES

Ethan Rutherford · *Farthest South & Other Stories* · USA

Bob Trammell · *The Origins of the Avant-Garde in Dallas & Other Stories* · USA